Thank You
for Being You

Thank You
for Being You

BRADLEY TREVOR GREIVE

**Andrews McMeel
Publishing, LLC**

Kansas City

10 11 12 TWP 10 9 8 7 6 5 4 3

ISBN-13: 978-0-7407-7649-6
ISBN-10: 0-7407-7649-5

PHOTO CREDITS
NIGEL DENNIS / AFRICA IMAGERY • www.africaimagery.com
JEAN-MICHEL LABAT / AUSCAPE • www.auscape.com.au
THEO ALLOFS / AUSCAPE • www.auscape.com.au
CORBIS AUSTRALIA PTY LTD • www.corbis.com
EMERALD CITY IMAGES • www.emeraldcityimages.com.au
GETTY IMAGES • www.gettyimages.com
JUPITER IMAGES • www.jupiterimages.com.au
ALISON BARNES MARTIN / MASTERFILE • www.masterfile.com
DANIEL J. COX / NATURAL EXPOSURES • www.naturalexposures.com
PETE OXFORD / NATUREPL.COM • www.naturepl.com
PAVEL GERMAN / WILDLIFE IMAGES • www.australiannature.com
PHOTOLIBRARY • www.photolibrary.com
PREMIUM • www.premiumnatur.de
WILDLIGHT PHOTO AGENCY • www.wildlight.net

Detailed page credits for the remarkable photographers whose work appears in *Thank You for Being You* and other books by Bradley Trevor Greive are freely available at www.btgstudios.com.

www.andrewsmcmeel.com

ATTENTION: SCHOOLS AND BUSINESSES
Andrews McMeel books are available at quantity discounts with bulk purchase for educational, business, or sales promotional use. For information, please write to: Special Sales Department, Andrews McMeel Publishing, LLC, 1130 Walnut Street, Kansas City, MO 64106.

For Siimon Reynolds.

Compassionate champion.

Beloved swine.

True friend.

ACKNOWLEDGMENTS

If I had one genuinely passionate regret (alas, I have hundreds) it would be that I don't thank the important people in my life nearly enough. Okay, to be fair, not being able to instantly articulate a devastatingly witty riposte in order to cripple my pedestrian adversaries with humiliation before they drift out of earshot would have to run a close second. But saying a simple and sincere "thank you" to those people whose mere existence, let alone selfless acts of kindness and understanding, have made my life so much better is something I wish I could do more of. After all, this is so pathetically easy to do.

Take this little book, for example, or the entire Blue Day Book series as a whole, for that matter. Though I am happy to soak up as much greasy, custard-rich credit as possible, the truth is that I would still be an oppressed member of the world's creative underclass, licking empty pizza boxes, fighting my fellow inebriates for pennies, and competing in poetry slams, were it not for the benevolent host who propelled me upward and onward.

To that end I would like to say how grateful I am to everyone who has supported, encouraged, and tolerated me over the years, starting with family members, friends, readers, and every member of my team at BTG Studios in Australia, past and present. I also want to thank each of my publishers, editors, translators, and booksellers scattered across the globe like jewels in the sand, among whom Chris Schillig would be the Hope Diamond (unless of course there is a bigger and more radiant diamond somewhere, in which case she is that one instead). I also want to acknowledge all the photographers with whom I have collaborated, and their agents, who have been so generous with their time and genius (*for a free, updated listing of photographic credits, please go to www.btgstudios.com*).

Most of all I want to thank Sir Albert J. Zuckerman, the man who, toward the end of last century, took an "ugly duckling" under his wing and stuffed its greedy, gaping gullet with love and wisdom until, to everyone else's astonishment, I emerged as the plump and somewhat celebrated goose that I am today.

With a childhood summer of sun-drenched days it becomes increasingly difficult to look back at the golden glow and identify just one standout moment worthy of special mention. So I find myself similarly embarrassed for choice when it comes to thanking Al profusely for all he has done to give me a better life and, more importantly, make me a better person.

Where to begin? There is nobody quite like Al, and so many memories of his physical and moral courage rush the page as one: The knife fight near Toulouse, France, where he bested a furious and unrepentant shoe salesman at a country market. The time we avoided being taken hostage outside a bookstore in Curitiba, Brazil, by hiding in the ladies' loo (his idea), and then, again, on the wrong side of the Argentinian border, when he convinced a pistol-waving customs official that the bedraggled sloth hidden under my shirt was actually a leaking colostomy bag so I could convey the poor creature to safety. The stormy night on board a bird-watching vessel many miles off the New Zealand coast, when he deliberately battered and split his noble brow against the timber headboard in his state room, so he could be flown to Sydney for emergency medical treatment just to slip away with some pilfered Band-Aids and a fistful of gauze to attend a glitzy function in my honour. And I will always remember the legendary Saxon Hausen dinner in Frankfurt when, with Al cheering me on while thumping my middle and lower back like a Taiko drum, I managed to consume not one but two gigantic veal schnitzels, each dense enough to choke a Doberman pinscher.

I could easily fill a book with Al's guardian angel heroics, and perhaps one day I shall, but well beyond the glittering world of international publishing awards and the inevitable kung-fu death matches, what I am actually most grateful to Al for has been the quiet optimism he has installed in my heart—no doubt gently gifted to me during the innumerable special moments we have shared over the years, many of which involved nothing more glamorous or dramatic than fresh coffee, newspapers, soft laughter, and perhaps an onion bagel.

If our tremendous journey comes to an end, and I suppose one day it must, then it will be these quiet, happy hours blurred beautifully into a radiant haze of love and friendship that will put a smile on my face and tears on my cheeks. And for that, dear sweet Albert, I thank you from the bottom of my heart.

When I think about you, I immediately realize
I have a lot to be grateful for. I really do.

I have filed away at least a million things to thank you for,
but somehow I never quite got around to actually telling you
what I felt nearly as often as I wanted to.

Now, I don't want to appear needy

or crowd you with mushy sentiment.

I just want to look you in the eye and finally say,

"Thank you".
Hang on, that was a bit feeble. What I meant to say was,

"THANK YOU!"

Whew, that feels better already. Let me just take a few deep breaths and centre myself. Okay, here we go.

Thank you for all the little things
you have done to make me smile

and basically feel good about myself.

Thank you for the great conversations we've shared
about important issues of global consequence,
and nothing much at all.

Thank you for all the delicious meals we have enjoyed

and for just being good company.

Thank you for all the little things you do to brighten my day—
knowing exactly when to pop in and say hi,

rubbing suntan lotion on my back without getting sand in it,

and showing me how to get around those accursed fish forks.

Thank you for being so thoughtful.
You always seem to put me first.

And I love it that you always remember my birthday
and pretend to forget my age.

I can't tell you how much I appreciate the way
you put up with my nitpicking, whining, and little tantrums,

19

and the fact that I tell my jokes back to front
so there is no punch line. Then I make you wait
while I try to tell it again, and I still get it wrong.

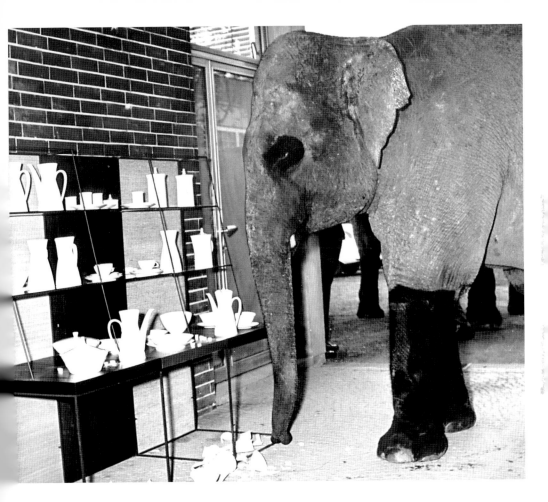

Thank you for ignoring both my general clumsiness
and the awkward moments that follow my little disasters.

Thank you for letting me know when overfed pigeons
are flying overhead.

Thank you for motivating me to get off my backside—

I wouldn't see or do half as much without you.

Thank you for getting me revved up and excited
about all the possibilities life has to offer

and for calming me down when it all gets to be a little too much.

Thank you for making a real effort
when we go out for a night on the town.
I feel fantastic when we are out together having fun.

And no matter how close to death I feel the next morning—
it is always worth it.

Of course, it's not just little things. There are some big things, too, and these are even harder to talk about. 29

Thank you for finding it in your heart to forgive me
for the things I have done that hurt or upset you.

Thank you for always telling me the truth straight up—
whether it be good news or bad.

Thank you for having the courage and compassion
not to run away screaming when you see me before 8 a.m.

Thank you for going along with my crazy dreams—

and for helping me imagine my name up in lights.

You always make me feel like a superstar.

Thank you for helping me come out of my shell,

for showing me there is a life to be had
outside my job and my home,

for helping me see the good things
that are sitting right in front of my nose,

and for teaching me how to laugh and have a great time
no matter where I am.

Thank you for helping me shrug off my emotional baggage

and for not ridiculing my nutty phobias, weird obsessions,
and general craziness.

Thank you for always looking out for me and my best interests

and for encouraging me to eat well, take good care of myself,

keep track of my pennies, and plan for the future.

Thank you for taking my fears seriously.
I am so grateful you are my port in the storm,

dashing to my side in my darkest hour

and helping me take a few baby steps back toward the light.

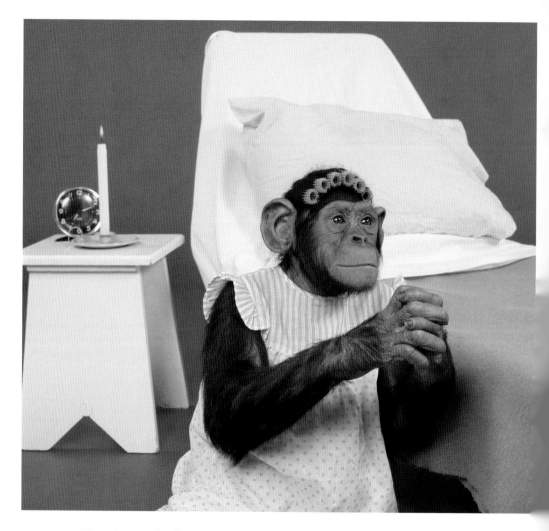

Thank you for keeping me in your heart and in your prayers,

for your quiet words of encouragement,

and for not letting me walk away without at least
one more compliment than I deserve.

Thank you for being someone
whom I can trust with my most fragile feelings.

Thank you for making me feel safe, comfortable, and happy whenever I am around you because of all the things you do and, I suppose, all the things you *never* do.

Thank you for not calling me before noon on Sundays

or any time during "Eastenders".

Thank you for not talking over me when we disagree.

And when I don't understand something, I am so grateful
you don't stare at me like I am an idiot

O.R S.P.E.A.K S.L.O.W.L.Y A.N.D L.O.U.D.L.Y
L.I.K.E I A.M A C.O.M.P.L.E.T.E M.O.R.O.N.

Er, gosh. I know I've forgotten so many fantastic things
I wanted to thank you for. Think, think, think!

Oh well. I could never list every wonderful thing you've done anyway, because you've gone out on a limb for me countless times.

Even if I could, mere words of thanks would always be inadequate.
I wish there was a better way to show you how I feel.

In a world full of fakes, you are the real thing. A true friend.

I feel so blessed—of all the billions of people
who could have shared my path, I stumbled across you.

Every kindness you have shown me has touched my heart.

Your generosity has made so many otherwise ordinary days
feel exciting and new.

I treasure every sweet gesture, every little thing you do.

Your example has opened up a window into my soul
that lets in the sunshine.

Thanks to your gift of friendship I can let go of shadows in the past,

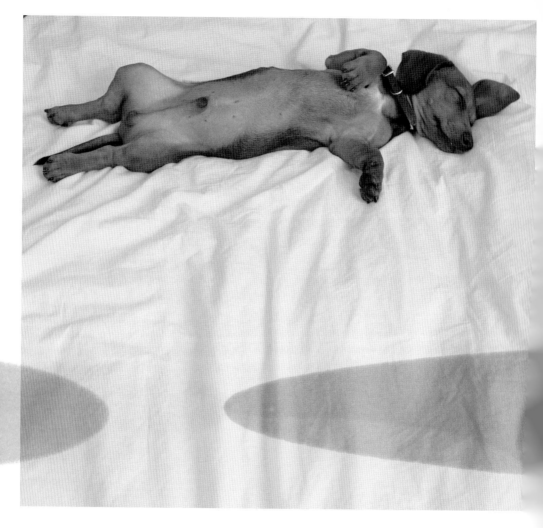

feel happy in my own skin,

and look forward to many bright, happy days ahead.
And so, in closing, I just want to say,

"Thank youuuuuuuuu!!!"

You're quite simply the best.